Learning with

Jesus

Text copyright © Claire Musters 2014
The author asserts the moral right
to be identified as the author of this work

Published by
The Bible Reading Fellowship
15 The Chambers, Vineyard
Abingdon OX14 3FE
United Kingdom
Tel: +44 (0)1865 319700
Email: enquiries@brf.org.uk
Website: www.brf.org.uk
BRF is a Registered Charity

ISBN 978 1 84101 692 4

First published 2014
10 9 8 7 6 5 4 3 2 1 0

Acknowledgments
Unless otherwise stated, scripture quotations are taken from The Holy Bible, New International
Version® Anglicised, NIV® Copyright © 1979, 1984, 2011 by www.biblica.com, Biblica, Inc.®
Used by permission. All rights reserved worldwide.

Scripture quotations taken from the Contemporary English Version of the Bible, published by
HarperCollins Publishers, are copyright © 1991, 1992, 1995 American Bible Society.

Cover photo: iStockphoto/Thinkstock

Every effort has been made to trace and contact copyright owners for material used in this
resource. We apologise for any inadvertent omissions or errors, and would ask those concerned
to contact us so that full acknowledgment can be made in the future.

A catalogue record for this book is available from the British Library

Printed and bound by CPI Group (UK) Ltd, Croydon, CR0 4YY

Learning with  Foundations21
the new way to do discipleship

Jesus

A seven-week course of study material
for individuals and groups

Claire Musters

Dedication and acknowledgments

I'd like to dedicate this book to my mother, whose unwavering faith is a constant source of inspiration to me. She has met with Jesus and found him to be the source of everything she needs, even in the midst of pain. She is also a fantastic proofreader and painstakingly read through the manuscript before I sent it off to the publisher. Thanks, Mum.

Thanks too to Steve, my husband, for his support and encouragement, which showed me I could write this book! His last-minute comments just before I sent the book to BRF were also invaluable.

Contents

Introduction

Love him or hate him, Jesus can elicit a strong response from people. Seen as a radical figure, a great scholar and teacher and/or the Son of God, he still makes waves in society today.

When Jesus came to earth more than 2000 years ago, many questions about life were raised, such as: what does he want with us? Where is God? What is life really about? Why should I bother about my neighbour? People are still asking these questions today, and Jesus is still relevant. Some of us receive him with faith and believe that he is who he said he was and that he died and rose again in order to bring us our only means of reconciliation to God.

This book takes a closer look at Jesus, covering both his divine and his human aspects—what he did and said while on earth, how he affected everyone he met, and what he expected from his disciples and other followers. This will all be approached in the context of what this means for us as disciples living in the 21st century.

How to use this book

The book is divided into seven sections, each covering one week. Each week begins with a general introduction (Day 1), which is also the material for the group meeting (if you are working through this in a group setting) as you begin each new week together. This meeting can be at any time that suits your group. Around six to eight people are ideal, but you can decide what would work for your own particular group. You will need access to a computer for the meetings, as well as on the other days if at all possible, as there is sometimes online material to look up. If you are using a laptop, you can plug it into a domestic flat-screen TV for a larger picture.

It is best to have a group leader to ensure that the meetings keep on track. He or she can also take notes of discussions and remember to refer back to any challenge you agree to try out during the week, any thoughts that you may wish to look at again and/or any prayer requests that have been voiced. The details of this are up to you, as is the length of your group meeting, although I would suggest keeping it to one-and-a-half to two hours.

There are also optional daily sections for individual participants to read and ponder (Days 2–5). Each contains reflections/questions to work through. Ideally, each person should have access to a copy of this book. You may also find it beneficial to pair up so that you have someone to check progress with regularly throughout the seven weeks.

Finally, there are special Saturday and Sunday activities that are best done on those particular days. The Saturday section suggests a 'community' activity that you could do together (sometimes with others in your church/neighbourhood/workplace) and the one for Sunday is more of a reflective activity.

You may decide that your group meeting is best held on a Wednesday. You would therefore start with Day 1 on the Wednesday, with individual group members looking at Days 2 and 3 on their own. You would then break on the Saturday and Sunday to focus on those specific activities, then go back to complete Days 4 and 5 individually on the Monday and Tuesday before coming together again for the next group meeting the following Wednesday.

It is also possible, of course, simply to use the Day 1 group material, or to draw more flexibly from any of the material in the book. Another alternative is to use the Saturday 'community' material for a midweek meeting.

The material included in this book is based on BRF's Foundations21 website resource, which has 3500 pages of content and is organised into 'rooms' that cover different aspects of Christian discipleship. The material is arranged in four distinct pathways (Matthew, Mark, Luke and John) that represent different learning styles, so that each person can access the information in the learning style that best suits them. This book utilises material from each of the pathways to ensure that it is accessible to everyone. Every subject that is covered here can also be explored in further depth on the website (see www.foundations21.net), with particular reference to the 'Jesus' room.

A page for this book has been created on the Foundations21 website. This contains all the weblinks referenced in the book. Simply go to www.foundations21.net/jesus. Group activities for each Day 1 session can also be found here.

You do not need to be logged in to Foundations21 to view this page, but for further study it is worth registering with www.foundations21.net, which gives you full access to the website and is quick, easy and free.

Week 1
Jesus the Messiah

Overview

During this week we will be concentrating on learning about Jesus the Messiah. Jesus is the fulfilment of the Old Testament, the promised Messiah—'chosen one' or saviour—who had been anticipated for generations. Here we are going to look at how he fulfils that role, and what type of messiah Jesus is. He certainly wasn't the saviour that the Jews had been expecting.

Day 1 (group session)

Before we begin looking at Jesus the Messiah, we are going to start with an individual task. Write a short description of what Jesus means to you as you embark on this course. Include any aspect about Jesus that you would like to learn more about. Now spend time sharing your descriptions together as a group. It would be a good idea for the group leader to make a note of what is said, so that you can refer back to people's thoughts later, whenever it is relevant to do so.

Now take a look at what Simon Thomas said about Jesus: www.foundations21.net/jesus

The king of kings

Throughout the New Testament there are references to Jesus being the Messiah. People asked whether he could indeed be the one they had been waiting for, although they were also often confused when they saw what he did and who he spent time with. Yet the Bible makes it clear that Jesus is indeed the Messiah king that the Jews were desperate for.

Question

How important is it for you to know that Jesus is the Messiah? Explain your answer to the group.

The Messianic tradition

The Old Testament made it clear that certain things would mark out the coming of a Saviour:

- It said he would be a descendant of David. The Gospel of Matthew's genealogy demonstrates this (see Matthew 1:1–17).
- It said he would be born in Bethlehem. The Gospel writers remind their readers that he was (see Matthew 2:1 and Luke 2:1–7).
- It said that he would be called a Saviour. The name 'Jesus' means 'saviour' (see Matthew 1:21).

Jesus is also called the 'son of David'. David was remembered as Israel's most successful king, as he had made the nation peaceful and prosperous. By now that was an Old Testament story passed down. The Jews had grown hungry for a new David, a leader who would make them great again and give them fresh hope.

So the title 'son of David' is not just about ancestry. It is a job description. Through Jesus, the kingly power of God was to be made known in Israel. That is why he was called 'Messiah'. The English word 'messiah' comes from the Hebrew *masiah*, which literally means 'anointed', a person marked out by God for a special task. In Greek—the language that Matthew used—the word for 'anointed' is our word 'Christ'. Jesus Christ was God's anointed leader, a new David, the shepherd king who would show the loving rule of God.

Question

How are you discovering Jesus to be 'the one I've been looking for' (another meaning of the word 'messiah') at this time? Share your thoughts with the group.

Group activities

Split into smaller groups of three or four and take a look at Isaiah 53. This is one of the Old Testament passages often referred to as a foretelling of what Jesus would accomplish during his time on earth. Spend time unpicking the language used and answer the following questions:

11

- What are the characteristics of Jesus that you recognise in this passage?
- Does this passage sound like a description of a messianic king? If not, why not?

We have already seen that there are passages in the Old Testament that point towards Jesus as the Messiah, prophesying (foretelling) where he would be from and what would happen to him. There are many others, echoed in the New Testament, and some are included below. Take a look through them as a group.

- The Messiah's throne will be anointed and eternal: Psalm 45:6–7 and Luke 1:33
- A messenger will prepare the way for the Messiah: Isaiah 40:3–5 and Luke 3:3–6
- The Messiah would be rejected by his own people: Isaiah 53:3 and John 1:11
- The Messiah would heal the broken-hearted: Isaiah 61:1–2 and Luke 4:18–19
- The Messiah would be seated at God's right hand: Psalm 110:1 and Mark 16:19

Day 2

The New Testament declares Jesus the Messiah

The New Testament often refers to Jesus' kingly status. The writers of this section were drawing, as we noted, on the messianic tradition of the Old Testament. As the second person of the Trinity (Father, Son and Holy Spirit), Jesus is the Son of God, and, being in the ancestral line of David, also the son of David. It is in the person of Jesus Christ, then, that the images of human and divine kingship are uniquely merged.

In the Gospels Jesus is called 'son of David', 'king of the Jews' or 'king of Israel', primarily by his opponents during his trial before Pilate. Take some time to look up the following passages: Matthew 2:2; Mark 10:47; Mark 15:32; Luke 23 and John 18—19.

Unusually, Jesus acknowledged his kingship openly in response to the high priest: 'I am [the Messiah], and you will see the Son of Man sitting at the right hand of the Mighty One and coming on the clouds of heaven' (Mark 14:62).

The culmination of Jesus Christ's kingship is found in Revelation. Here he is the 'King of kings and Lord of lords' (see Revelation 19:16).

Reflections

- What new things have you learned about Jesus the Messiah today?
- Close your eyes and try to imagine Jesus seated on his throne, at the right hand of God. Try to describe the emotions you feel as you do this. Are you terrified, in awe, happy, confident?

Day 3

An unexpected type of king

The Jews expected their Messiah to come as a mighty warrior to defeat their oppressors, the Romans. Watch the trailer for *Batman Begins* at www.foundations21.net/jesus. Do you think it was this type of vigilante, legendary figure that the Jews were hoping for?

Rob Frost writes about Jesus' birth in *Jesus in the Third Millennium* (BRF, 2000):

The angel told the shepherds that the baby born in a manger in Bethlehem was 'Christ the Lord'. It must have been a confusing message. Who would have expected 'the Lord' to be born in a lowly stable?

Jesus came to show that being Lord in the kingdom of God was very different from the kingship we have created as humans. Indeed, he never defended himself, or attacked the Romans in the way the Jews wanted him to. And his 'triumphal entry' into Jerusalem during the feast of Passover consisted of his riding on a borrowed donkey—see Matthew 21, noting the way Jesus is fulfilling Old Testament scripture here (Zechariah 9:9) and also the way he is referred to as the son of David again. In the days he walked the earth as a human no one fully knew who Jesus was; it took the resurrection and the descent of the Spirit to reveal his full majesty and wonder.

Reflections

- Try to put yourself in the shoes of a New Testament Jew. How do you think it must have felt to be confronted with such a different type of messiah from the one you were expecting?
- Thank God that, even though it may be confusing to our human minds, his plans and purposes were fully worked out in Jesus' life and death.

Day 4

The servant king

We have already seen that Jesus was not the military warrior that many had been longing for. Indeed, he came to model an utterly different way of living: serving others. Because of this he is often referred to as the servant king. (Acts has many mentions of him as a servant: see Acts 3:13, 26; 4:27, 30.)

Jesus tried to teach others to live this way too: '"You know that the rulers of the Gentiles lord it over them, and their high officials exercise authority over them. Not so with you. Instead, whoever wants to become great among you must be your servant, and whoever wants to be first must be your slave—just as the Son of Man did not come to be served, but to serve, and to give his life as a ransom for many"' (Matthew 20:25–28).

Jesus knew that in order to save humanity he had to suffer at the hands of the very people he had come to save. During his trial, he explains: '"My kingdom is not of this world. If it were, my servants would fight to prevent my arrest by the Jewish leaders. But now my kingdom is from another place"' (John 18:36).

Jesus also refers to himself as 'the good shepherd': '"I am the good shepherd. The good shepherd lays down his life for the sheep"' (John 10:11). Shepherds are responsible for their sheep and look after them in all weather conditions, often putting themselves in danger to make sure each individual sheep is safe.

Reflections

- Ponder the idea of Jesus being the good shepherd. What does that mean to you personally?
- How can you serve those around you practically today, to live out Jesus' teaching?

Day 5

The secret Messiah?

Mark's Gospel describes many instances of Jesus forbidding people to say who he is. It is as if Jesus wants to keep the fact that he is the Messiah secret, but why?

Mark says that Jesus 'would not let the demons speak because they knew who he was' (1:34). Obviously, demons were unreliable, evil witnesses, but Jesus also told many people he healed not to say what he had done. The first reason scholars give for this was that it was not yet time for his ministry to be widely known. Perhaps he was concerned his fame would spread too rapidly. Indeed, in the account of Jesus turning water into wine at a wedding Jesus says: '"Why do you involve me? … My hour has not yet come"' (John 2:4).

A second reason appears to be that he would be unable to travel freely in the towns, making it more difficult to reach people who couldn't go to the countryside to hear him preach. In Mark 1:40–45 Jesus heals a leper and instructs him not to tell anyone, but the leper was unable to contain himself. As a result, Jesus could no longer enter a town openly.

The final reason, which we have already touched upon, is that first-century Jews had too many misconceptions about who the Messiah was. Jesus wanted to avoid people getting the wrong idea about him.

Reflections

- Jesus kept his true identity secret from most people but still expected them to trust and follow him. Are there any areas in your life in which God asks you to trust him without explaining?
- Can you think of times when it would be better not to speak out? Lay your hand on your lips and ask God to impart wisdom so that you may know what should be said, and when, and to whom.

Saturday

Community activity

Many people today like to view Jesus simply as a signpost to God, or a teacher of timeless truths, rather than the Messiah. Brainstorm some ways in which you think you could practically show those you come into contact with that Jesus is indeed your Messiah—and what impact this has on your life.

For example, you could practise being open about the fact that you go to church, and why, when asked on a Monday morning what you did at the weekend.

Sunday

Reflective activity

Think about the various aspects of Jesus' messiahship that we have touched upon. Which one has had the most impact on you this week? You could do some more research into that area (see www.foundations21.net/jesus). End by thanking God for sending Jesus as the Messiah to our world.

Review

We have seen over the last five days that Jesus is indeed the Messiah, but that he did not come in the way the Jews were expecting. Although his life fulfilled much Old Testament prophecy, they were so desperate for someone to save them from Roman oppression that many missed the significance of his coming.

Jesus certainly didn't play by the usual standards and rules. His kingship comes from another kingdom—the kingdom of God—and, as we've explored, that means it isn't about crushing enemies and sitting back while others serve him. Jesus the Messiah came as a suffering servant, to offer himself as a sacrifice for us. What an amazing, humble king!

Week 2
The divine nature of Jesus

Overview

It can be quite overwhelming to consider how Jesus was both fully man and fully God. This week we will be focusing on how Jesus Christ encapsulated the deity of God while here on earth, and what that means for us today. Next week we will look at his humanity.

Day 1 (group session)

There from the beginning

Look up John 1:1–4 together and ask someone to read it aloud. These verses call Jesus the Word of God, a phrase you will be looking at in greater detail in your individual study during Day 2. But the importance of these verses is that they remind us that Jesus existed from the very beginning of time. Not only was Jesus with God, Jesus *was* God. This is a difficult, yet vital, concept to grasp, as it establishes the inseparable nature of Jesus and the living creator God.

A creative force

The verses in John state that 'Nothing was made without the Word. Everything that was created received its life from him, and his life gave light to everyone' (vv. 3–4, CEV). Here John was making what seemed like an outrageous claim: Jesus is the creator. But, more than that, it is Jesus who reveals the very purpose of human life. John is stating that in each part of our lives, whatever highs and lows we face, Jesus was and is at the point of origin. Every facet of life—like a jewel with a thousand faces to catch the light—owes its meaning to the person of Jesus Christ.

Show some images of creation from the internet.

Questions

Get into small groups of two or three to answer the following questions:

* How did the images make you feel? Do they help you to realise that the Jesus we have been talking about, our Messiah, was there right at the beginning of time?

- What do you 'see' spiritually when you look at the 'wonders of the natural world'? Where is Jesus in what you see?

Group activity

Read through Genesis 1. You will see that the text talks about God, and also the Spirit of God hovering over the earth before anything was formed in it. Take some time now, close your eyes and try to picture Jesus there at the creation of the world. You could even read the passage again inserting 'Jesus' where it says 'God' to make the connection easier.

Jesus is 100 per cent God

During his time on earth, Jesus proved his divine nature time and time again. As we saw when we looked at Jesus the Messiah, one of the ways he did this was by fulfilling Old Testament prophecy. And not only did he proclaim who he was when asked directly during his trial, but his disciples also made the claim that he was the Son of God and the creator of all.

Group activity

Spend some time together looking up the following verses and focus on what they tell you about Jesus' divinity:

- Luke 7:22 (Jesus was able to perform miracles)
- Matthew 16:13–17 (His disciples recognised his perfect life and received revelation of who he truly was)
- Luke 24:44 (Jesus fulfilled prophecy)
- John 10:30–38; Mark 14:61–64 (While he didn't do it often, Jesus did identify himself as being one with God)
- Hebrews 1:8 (quoting Psalm 45:6), Colossians 1:16; John 12:40 (quoting Isaiah 6:10) (The claims of his disciples)

Power over death

Of course one of the biggest pointers to Jesus' divinity is the resurrection. He took on the full force of God's wrath and humanity's evil and then came to life again. What a powerful witness!

Group activity

Read the following verses:

- Mark 8:31 (Jesus explains to his followers what must happen)
- Luke 24:39 (After the resurrection, Jesus urges his disciples to believe that he really is standing before them)
- Acts 17:16–34 (Paul teaches about the resurrection)

It was through his resurrection that Jesus established his deity once and for all but also made it possible for us to have our sins forgiven and come into a right relationship with God. Spend some time together praying, thanking Jesus for his divinity and for the way he sacrificed himself, fighting and overcoming the powers of darkness, so that we could be reconciled to the Father.

Day 2

The living Word of God

Here we are going to concentrate further on Jesus being the living Word of God. Start by reading John 1:1–18.

You could say the following prayer:

God, please help me to open my eyes
so that I can truly see Jesus,
and know him as the living Word of God.
Amen

At the beginning of his Gospel, John uses the Greek term *logos*, which is translated as 'word' or 'reason' (the divine reason behind the universe). We can see both Jewish and Greek elements within Christianity, and John fused them together in his Gospel. He starts by uniquely identifying Jesus with the divine *logos*, which combines the Jewish idea of God's self-expression with the Greek concept of the 'reason', the creative force that began the universe.

Reflections

- In what ways is it helpful to you to know that Jesus is the one through whom all things were made (see v. 3)?
- If you want to find out more about the term *logos*, visit the Foundations21 website (see www.foundations21.net/jesus for a list of sites that go into more details of John's theology of Jesus as the *logos* of God).

Day 3

Jesus, the Son of God

The Old Testament uses the phrase 'son/s of God' in three ways: to refer to angels (Genesis 6:2), Israel (Exodus 4:22–23), and the king—often understood as 'David's son'—who would establish the foundations of God's temple (2 Samuel 7:12–14) and who had been handed the authority from God to judge and rule his people. Jesus would have identified most with this third meaning.

People in Jesus' time may also have picked up on the Greek use of the term 'son of God', which referred to the idea of a 'divine man'—someone who was human but possessed divine power and the ability to work miracles. In the New Testament and later Christian thought, the 'son of God' title was used to acknowledge Jesus as God. This is particularly expressed in John's Gospel.

- Jesus perfectly obeys his Father's will (John 4:34; 5:30; 6:38; 7:28; 8:29, 42)
- He shares his Father's work (John 5:17–19, 21, 24; 6:40; 9:4; 10:37–38)
- He says nothing except what he has heard from the Father (John 3:32–4; 12:49–50; 15:15) and does nothing except what he has seen the Father do (John 5:19–20; 8:38)
- He enjoys intimate fellowship with the Father (John 1:18; 4:22–3; 6:45–7; 8:55; 14:13–16; 15:15; 16:15)

All of this implies that the divine sonship of Jesus is unique; he is Son of God in a sense not true of anyone else.

Reflection

- Thinking about all the elements the title 'son of God' contains, choose one you would like to focus on learning more about today.

Day 4

The beloved of God

The relationship of the Father with his Son is one of real beauty. Jesus himself was conscious of this, addressing his Father in prayer using the intimate name of *Abba* (see Mark 14:36). The love between them is revealed in many New Testament scriptures. Look up John 3:35; 5:20; 10:17; 17:23 for examples of how the Father loves the Son.

'My beloved Son'

Perhaps the most poignant example of God's love for Jesus is revealed during Jesus' baptism. Read Matthew 3:13–17, imagining yourself as a bystander at the time. What an amazing sight to see the Holy Spirit descend upon Jesus like a dove, and for all to hear the voice of heaven declaring his love! The depth of love and pride he has for his Son is summed up in his words, '"This is my Son, whom I love; with him I am well pleased"' (v. 17).

One of the reasons why God was so pleased with him was his total obedience to doing the will of God.

Reflections

- If you are a parent, try to think back to a moment when you were intensely proud of your child. That is just a tiny taste of how much the Father loves the Son.
- The Bible clearly says that we are now God's children—we can call him *Abba*, Father (Romans 8:15; Galatians 4:6). Drink in that truth and spend some time drawing close to your 'daddy'.
- Have you been baptised? If not, spend some time today looking into why Christian congregations actively encourage this (good starting points are Matthew 28:19 and 2 Corinthians 5:17).

Day 5

Equality with God

Jesus' sense of unique sonship went further than just a close filial relationship to God. The intimacy that existed between them meant that Jesus alone was qualified to reveal God to humanity, because he *was* God. Even Satan and the demons acknowledged Jesus' status: 'The devil said, "If you are God's Son, jump off. The Scriptures say: 'God will give his angels orders about you. They will catch you in their arms, and you won't hurt your feet on the stones'"' (Matthew 4:6, CEV).

While Jesus was often reticent to speak about his unique equality with God, there are instances in the Bible that show he knew his standing and purpose on earth (see John 10:30–33; 12:44–46). He had God's authority, which was revealed in the wisdom he spoke, the miracles he performed and, ultimately, in his death and resurrection, after which he ascended into heaven to sit at God's right hand (Ephesians 1:20).

Reflections

- What did you learn about Jesus' equality with God through the verses cited above?
- Take a sheet of paper, write the word 'equality' at the top of it, then spend some time writing down all the words and phrases that you associate with it.
- Now work back through your list; how many of these words do you think Jesus fulfilled? Do you think he was a unique example of equality? Why?
- Now look at Philippians 2:5–7. How do you respond to the call from Paul and Timothy to imitate Christ's humility?

Saturday

Community activity

Spend some time thinking about the fact that Jesus *is* God. In John 14:6 he clearly said: "'I am the way and the truth and the life. No one comes to the Father except through me.'" What is it about your faith that reveals this truth to those around you? To demonstrate the same servant-hearted attitude that Jesus had, think of simple, kind ways you can serve those you see daily; perhaps offering to make them a cup of tea or helping them with a task.

Sunday

Reflective activity

Has the idea of Jesus being both fully divine and fully human at the same time baffled you in the past? Think back over the last five days and pick out the one thing that you feel has cemented your knowledge about Jesus' divine nature. Write down this truth in your journal (if you keep one), on your phone or on a piece of paper next to your desk and meditate on it for a few moments each time you see it.

Review

Jesus came to earth as the Word becoming flesh. While he walked upon the earth as a human being, he was unique in that he was still divine. He was there at the beginning of time, in perfect relationship with the Father and Spirit, and chose to obey the will of God and come in human form for a time. This was the only way for us to be reconciled to the Father; without his divine nature Jesus would never have been able to fulfil his mission here on earth.

Week 3
Jesus' humanity

Overview

As we have seen, Jesus was fully God, and yet he was also fully human. This week we are going to concentrate on looking more closely at his human characteristics, and why it was so important for him to become flesh and blood in order to extend God's salvation to the whole of humanity.

Day 1 (group session)

Becoming human

Jesus of Nazareth has been described as 'God with a human face'. As a group, start your session by thinking about how you imagine God would look if he were to become human. Write down, or even draw, your thoughts.

Jesus of Nazareth contained the whole life of God in a human frame, which means that in the face of Jesus Christ we see the face of God (Colossians 1:15). In his life, words, acts and, most especially, his death and resurrection the entire saving work of God was present, although it was not immediately seen and recognised. So, although the grace of God comes first, it is only as we experience a living relationship with him that our acceptance of God's love can truly take place. And then the face of Jesus Christ begins to change our own faces, so that we reflect something of God in our lives.

Group activity

Get into smaller groups of two or three, and discuss the fact that the face of Christ changes our faces. (See 2 Corinthians 18.) How do you think that happens? Challenge one another to reflect on how much you think that has happened in your own lives.

Jesus has a place in history

Matthew was obviously keen to prove both Jesus' human and divine credentials, listing in his Gospel Jesus' extensive family tree, which went right back through David (the messianic line) to Abraham, the father of the nations (see Matthew 1). Luke's Gospel went even further, plotting his family tree right back to Adam (Luke

3:23–38). This places Jesus in time and history and, indeed, no serious scholar questions that Jesus existed as a historical figure.

So why did the Son of God become the Son of Man?

Galatians 4:4–5 says that 'when the set time had fully come, God sent his Son, born of a woman, born under the law, to redeem those under the law, that we might receive adoption to sonship.'

Take some time to look through the following reasons why Jesus came to earth as a human.

Jesus Christ became a human being...

- to reveal God to humanity (see 1 Timothy 3:16; Romans 1:19–20)
- to fulfil scripture (see Week 1, page 12)
- to be Israel's king (Matthew 2:1–2; John 12:12–16; also referencing Zechariah 9:9)
- to become our High Priest (Hebrews 2:17; 4:15; 7:11–25)
- to die on the cross for our redemption (Matthew 1:21; 20:28; Hebrews 2:5–9; 7:27)
- to be an example to believers of how they should live (John 13:15; 14:15–24; Philippians 2:5–11) NB His teachings gave specific principles to live by—we focus on these in Week 4.
- to defeat Satan (1 Corinthians 15:55; Hebrews 2:14; Revelation 1:18)

Questions

- Do you find it inspiring or challenging to think that Jesus was a real Middle Eastern man, rather than the radiant meek shepherd we see in many paintings?
- How does the fact that Jesus was fully human as well as divine challenge your faith?

Day 2

Characteristics of his humanity

We are told that Jesus was born as a human child and matured normally. He lived a simple life and took on the career of his father, becoming a carpenter.

Watch the following clip, which talks about the fact that Jesus was a real man: www.foundations21.net/jesus

Have you ever thought of Jesus laughing? Of his having strong, rough hands? Ponder the aspects of the video that struck you the most.

Here are some quotations about Jesus' humanity:

He was a builder, he was so magnetic and so winsome that thousands of people would leave their work daily to listen to him preaching.
MICHAEL GREEN

He was a real man in the very best sense of that word. He wasn't soft and pathetic but a real wild free awesome man.
PHIL DUNN

Jesus was open to the full range of human emotions. He displayed real anger, was easily moved by the suffering that he saw and found it very difficult to come to terms with his impending death.
MICHAEL KEENE

Reflections

- Do the quotations make Jesus' humanity more real to you?
- Look up the following passages, and think about the emotions Jesus displayed: John 11:1–45; Mark 11:12–26; Matthew 26:36–46. Imagine the scenes, using all your senses to build up a picture of them, and try to feel the emotions yourself.

Day 3

Why did Jesus *have* to become human?

The human race needed rescuing from its sin, but, as we can see from all the elaborate rituals the Israelites had to undertake to draw near to God's presence (for many examples, see Leviticus and Numbers), God's justice and holiness demanded a sacrifice. But a mere human couldn't act as rescuer as they would, by definition, be part of the problem. Someone who was 'merely' God would not be entitled to save us; he would not be one of us. Jesus became the answer: as 'God become flesh', he is *eligible* to save us and also has the *power* to save us.

Jesus can empathise with us

Look up Hebrews 2:18 and 4:15 and think about the following question: what is the difference between a God bellowing at us from a distance, and the God who cares?

Reflections

- Think about what you are struggling with most at the moment and invite Jesus into that situation/temptation to help you.
- Jesus was the character of God in a human body. What does that say about what you are meant to be like? What does it say about what you *are* like, when viewed by God, in the light of Jesus Christ?

Day 4

Did Jesus' humanity limit him?

Luke refers to Jesus' growing in wisdom (2:52), which implies he learned as we do. While Jesus always had a right to divine knowledge and could have used it, he only made use of this as he knew his heavenly Father wanted him to. Jesus allowed his obedience to his Father to limit both his power and his knowledge (see John 5:19–20 and 6:38).

What did it cost him?

Jesus made himself totally dependent on, and vulnerable to, the humanity that he had created. This happened when he was born, throughout his life and especially on the cross.

His ministry came at a huge cost to him. He had no fixed home, no family around him, and he faced much hostility. He spent his time travelling around on foot and by boat. He endured much hardship during his lifetime.

Reflections

- In the light of the above, try this imagination exercise. Jot down diary entries for one day of Jesus' life, filling in every hour.
- Jesus lived a life of complete obedience, doing only what God prompted him to do. Ponder how often in a usual day you ask God what he wants you to do.

Day 5

The Son of Man

We are looking specifically at this term because it is the one that Jesus himself used more than any other to refer to himself. In the Old Testament the phrase means simply 'man' (see Psalm 8:4, KJV), but the majority of contexts in which Jesus used the title indicate that he was thinking of Daniel 7:13–14, in which the 'son of man' is a heavenly figure. In the Jewish apocalyptic tradition this son of man is regarded as a pre-existent one who will come at the end of the ages as judge and as a light to the Gentiles, and Jesus refers to this during his trial (see Mark 14:62).

The title is used to refer to Jesus:

- to emphasise his authority and power (Mark 2:10, 28; Luke 12:8)
- to emphasise his humility (Mark 10:45; Luke 19:10)
- to emphasise his pre-existence, and descent into the world (John 3:13; 6:62–63)
- to reveal his role of uniting heaven and earth (John 1:51)
- to show he is coming to judge humanity (John 5:22–27)

Reflections

- If you are artistic, perhaps you could take some time to draw how you picture the vision in Daniel. Alternatively, simply meditate further on the passage.
- Why do you think that Jesus chose to use the term 'son of man' to refer to himself?

Saturday

Community activity

Jesus was a 1st-century Middle Eastern man who was viewed as a revolutionary—nothing like the blond-haired, blue-eyed man that we see in many paintings. In a group, search for the images for 'representations of Jesus' on the internet. Spend time discussing how they differ from what you think Jesus would have been like. Do this with other Christians as well as with those without faith if possible, to get a range of reactions.

Sunday

Reflective activity

Tom Wright, in his book *The Original Jesus* (Lion Hudson, 1997), writes: 'The true god is the God of sovereign love; and it's a contradiction in terms to suppose that love will remain uninvolved, or detached, or impersonal. The true God isn't a vaguely beneficial gas. He wears a human face, crowned with thorns.' How do you respond to this statement, in the light of what you've learned of Jesus' humanity?

Review

We have seen how Jesus was a real human being who grew up to live a simple life in Nazareth as a carpenter. He was the perfect example of obedient humanity, laying aside much of his majesty to put himself at the mercy of this earth. When he started his travelling ministry at the age of 30, he did only the things he knew his heavenly Father told him to do. He felt all the depth of emotions that we do, and was tempted in every way we are, which means that he is able to empathise with us in our personal struggles today.

Week 4
Jesus' teachings

Overview

There has been much written about the things that Jesus said while he walked this earth and, indeed, listening to what somebody says is the best way to get to know them. Here we are going to focus on what Jesus taught during his travelling ministry.

Day 1 (group session)

Jesus spent a lot of his time teaching during his three-year ministry. He taught both his small group of disciples and also much larger gatherings of the wider public.

Jesus was preparing his disciples for the life that they would lead after his death and resurrection. He was revealing more about the nature of God and teaching all who would listen about the way they should live.

Group activity

Can you think of three tough things that Jesus has taught you? Share them with the person sitting closest to you.

Why were his teachings seen as radical?

Look up Mark 1:21. Jesus spoke with great authority and amazed everyone around him, even at the tender age of twelve (see Luke 2:41–52, especially v. 47). Yet imagine for a moment how you would have felt if you had been a Jewish teacher of the Law and a young upstart began revealing things from the scriptures you had never seen. That must have stung! Jesus' wisdom and stature grew as he did (v. 52), and he continued to make the religious leaders uncomfortable as he challenged their traditions and way of doing things. The political establishment found him a threat because he taught with great authority and spoke of powers way beyond this world. Because of this, he was viewed as a radical and was ultimately condemned to death. And the Roman rulers found him mysterious, baffling and ultimately so confusing that they did not spare his life.

Jesus used parables

Jesus often used hard-hitting parables to teach his disciples and other listeners. Containing deep truths in such stories allowed them to penetrate people's hearts and minds, and it was a good way for people to remember them too. There is no one way to interpret these parables. Some are stories with one simple point— so if you uncover that point, you will have solved the mystery of the parable. Others are complex narratives with many shades and levels of meaning. Similarly, they can be seen as mainly addressing individuals then and now, or they can be heard as mainly having a social message for Jesus' day, which is still as relevant for society today as it was then.

Group activities

- Look at these three definitions of a parable. Discuss which one you find most helpful, and also talk about what you think the parables mean for you today:
  * A parable is a brief story that is true to life, comparing the point of commonality between two unlike things, given for the purpose of teaching spiritual truth
  * A parable is a short, simple story teaching a moral or spiritual lesson... from the Greek root word *parabole*, which literally means 'to throw beside'
  * A parable is a simple word-picture, which is used to help people understand who God is and what his kingdom or reign is like

- Many of Jesus' parables were used to teach about the kingdom of God. Discuss what you think this phrase means.
- Look at the webpage that includes a list of all Jesus' parables: www.foundations21.net/jesus. If you have time, look up one or two examples (avoiding the parable of the sower as you will be

focusing on it in the next couple of days). Try to unpack them as a group, to discover what Jesus is trying to teach you today.

- Discuss what you think the teachings of Jesus you have looked at today reveal to you of his character. What do they tell you about him?
- If you would like to, take a look at the website that contains some 'modern-day' examples of parables: www.foundations21. net/jesus. Read a couple and then comment on whether you find them effective.

Day 2

The parable of the sower

Start by watching an online video of this parable, which is found in Mark 4. You can find one on the internet by searching for 'parable of the sower video'.

Now let's take a closer look at what this parable could be saying. There are four types of ground in this story. Jesus reveals to his disciples that these stand for the four responses that people make to the gospel message. The sower does his work thoroughly enough and the seed is good, but the trouble lies with the soil. John Eddison, in his book *Newness of Life* (BRF, 1999, p. 27), describes the four different kinds of soil as follows:

- The light-hearted: these people hear the message of Christ. But before it sinks in, other things crowd in and snatch it away
- The faint-hearted: these people make a good start, but are not prepared for the opposition—verbal, if not physical—that Christians are likely to meet, and give up
- The half-hearted: there is a good start, but before long the cares and pleasures of the world grow up, take over the soil and smother the message
- The whole-hearted: this is a picture of a fruitful Christian who gives the message two things that the others deny it—root and room to grow

Reflection

- In what circumstances do you feel:
  - * downtrodden, like the road?
  - * shallow, like the rocky ground?
  - * pressurised, like the thorny ground?
  - * fruitful for God, like the good ground?

Day 3

Digging deeper

As we have seen, Jesus' parables often had different levels of meaning. Here is an example of the reaction Jesus' parable of the sower had from the people of the day. Read it as if it is a newspaper report from that time. You may find it helps if you can afterwards close your eyes and imagine the scenes of outrage.

Jesus rocks the political establishment

'This time he's gone too far!' That was the verdict of Reuben ben Judgin, government minister and one of the chief temple teachers, on hearing Jesus' latest political parable. 'Who does he think he is? Some kind of apocalyptic figure?' The cabinet minister delivered his diatribe on the steps of the outer temple court.

What has got the politicians so mad? To many it was simply a pleasant story about a farmer. Others saw it as a deep challenge to their own personal integrity. But to the religious lawyers, it was Jesus throwing down the gauntlet. The so-called 'parable of the broadcaster' is variously being described as 'an outrage', 'a mystery', 'a cleverly hidden time bomb' or 'the work of the devil'.

Reflections

- The Foundations21 website has further ideas about what this parable could mean, such as the soils being various moments in Israel's history. See www.foundations21.net/jesus
- Choose another parable to look at today, and ask God to reveal different levels of meaning to you.

Day 4

Sermon on the Mount

Start by reading Matthew 5—7. The teaching covered here is known as the Sermon on the Mount because Jesus gave it on a hill near Capernaum. He was drawing large crowds by this point, and the 'sermon' may well have lasted several days. In it, Jesus challenges attitudes and covers lifestyle issues such as money, anger, lust, love, prayer, fasting and worry.

Rather than a manual on how to be a Christian, this set of teachings is a description of what a Christian should naturally be like. Jesus starts with the Beatitudes, describing the characteristics of a Christian. Jesus then describes how a Christian should live within a hostile world, continuously aware of the presence of God.

Towards the end Jesus says: 'So in everything, do to others what you would have them do to you, for this sums up the Law and the Prophets' (7:12). By referring back, he seems to be summarising Old Testament commands. Here, in such a short phrase, he is providing a profound truth—if we all learned to treat others as we want to be treated, how much better the world would be!

Reflections

- Take a closer look at the Beatitudes and think about how they contradict the world's view about what makes a person blessed. Meditate on the one that speaks to you most.
- How have your words and deeds to others in the last week reflected how you yourself want to be treated?

Day 5

Teaching by example

We will look in closer detail at the things Jesus said to his disciples and expected of them in Week 7, but it is important to note here that after Jesus taught his disciples and others around him on the mountain, he went on to live out and demonstrate his teachings. In Matthew 8—9 Jesus teaches by example; in chapter 10 Jesus invites his close disciples to learn by example. The amazing thing is that those disciples then received his authority to do exactly as he did. They were no longer simply disciples (10:1), they were now Jesus' apostles (v. 2). They were sent to all the surrounding area, representing the twelve tribes of Israel. Their mission was to announce the kingdom of God by the way they taught. They, too, were to teach by example. Before his ascension, Jesus gave the great commission (see 28:16–20), giving all his followers the authority to teach in Jesus' name. Again, they taught by example.

Reflections

There are direct parallels between what Jesus did and the instructions that he gave his disciples. Look up the following and note the similarities:

- Matthew 9:36 and 10:6
- Matthew 9:35 and 10:7
- Matthew 8:1–4 and 10:8
- Matthew 8:28–34 and 10:8
- Matthew 8:14–17 and 10:8
- Matthew 9:24–5 and 10:8

Saturday

Community activity

Since the days of the early church in Jerusalem, every Christian group that has followed Jesus' teaching has authority to teach as Jesus taught, in obedience to Jesus' command (Matthew 28:20). The same pattern of teaching by example is to be part of every church today too. Spend some time together thinking about how well your church, and perhaps any small groups you attend, teaches by example. You might also want to think about whether 'older' Christians mentor younger ones effectively.

Sunday

Reflective activity

Jesus often made people uncomfortable with his teachings. He used parables that had hidden messages, but nevertheless cut straight to the heart on issues. Is there something among his teachings that causes you to feel uncomfortable? Perhaps you need to spend some time looking at why that is the case, and what you can do about it.

Review

Jesus' teachings are full of such richness that a week's worth of short reflections cannot possibly do them justice. However, we have seen how they reveal more about the character of God and that the people who follow him should reflect his character. At the time, Jesus' words cut deeply, sometimes causing great offence, particularly to the religious leaders who had constructed a whole series of elaborate rules and regulations for themselves and the people to follow. For this man, who spoke with such authority, to come and teach another way enraged them. And many have the same reaction today. Jesus' teachings are radical—and are supposed to challenge and upset our comfortable, self-constructed norms.

Week 5
Jesus' 'I am' sayings

Overview

Within his teachings Jesus also made many statements about himself, which are known as the 'I am' sayings. We are going to spend this week unpacking their significance for us as modern-day followers of Jesus.

Day 1 (group session)

Watch the video that is a montage of each of the 'I am' sayings: www.foundations21.net/jesus

The seven 'I am' sayings are:

- I am the light of the world
- I am the bread of life
- I am the gate
- I am the good shepherd
- I am the way, the truth and the life
- I am the resurrection
- I am the vine

Group activity

Take a look at the list above and brainstorm some ideas about why you think Jesus called himself each of these things. You may want to come back to these as you work through each 'I am' saying later in the week, to see how accurate you were.

The bread of life

Read the whole of John 6, perhaps getting each person to read a few verses out loud to the group. This chapter includes the first of Jesus' 'I am' sayings.

Now consider: Jesus had just performed two amazing miracles: feeding more than 5000 people with five loaves of bread and two fish, and walking on water. His statement 'I am the bread of life' (v. 35) comes in answer to the question what sign he was going to show the people to prove he had God's seal of approval. What sign did they need when he had just fed them all out of nearly nothing? They quote the Old Testament: 'Our ancestors ate the manna in the wilderness; as it is written: "He gave them bread from heaven to eat"' (v. 31; see Exodus 16 for the full story). By using the same imagery, Jesus was trying to teach the people that he is the source of unending nourishment, as God taught their ancestors back in the desert (Deuteronomy 8:3–5).

The response of the people revealed that they could not understand or accept that Jesus was saying he comes from heaven, because they knew where he had been born and had grown up. There is a need for faith in order to receive revelation from God on this.

When Jesus went on to explain that his body would be offered up to give the world life, and that they would need to feed on the bread—his body—they viewed it literally rather than seeing the metaphoric use of language. Jesus gives further explanation of why his claim to be the bread of life was far superior to the manna miracle. We can read John 6:57–58 in the light of what we know of Jesus' death and resurrection, but his original listeners would mostly have been baffled—and somewhat appalled—by the imagery used.

Why bread?

As a group, think about the significance of the use of the term 'bread', both for the Jews in Jesus' day and for us today. Here are some ideas to get your conversation started:

* Bread is a universal commodity
* Most countries in the world have some form of bread
* Even in ancient times they made bread
* Bread is associated with life, health, nourishment and prosperity
* When Jesus said 'I am the bread of life', he was making an exclusive claim. You can't get this kind of bread anywhere else
* Jesus died and rose again—the Communion we take regularly as Christians celebrates this

Group activity

Share bread and wine or grape juice together. Allow each person to tear their bread off the loaf so that they can look closely at it and remember Jesus' words that he is *the* bread of life. Pray together, thanking Jesus for his everlasting sustenance made available to all who believe.

Day 2

The light of the world

Begin by closing the curtains, then light a candle to see how it illuminates the area around it. Keep the candle burning as a focal point as you read on.

Read John 8:12–20. Jesus says he is the light of the world, again picking up on imagery people would recognise. Verse 20 says that he was where the offerings were put, which was also where candles burned to symbolise the pillar of fire that led the Israelites through the desert (see Exodus 13:21–22). But he was challenged by the Pharisees. Why? If Jesus is light, wouldn't everyone recognise that?

Evil has confused people's thoughts and vision. Without the power of God in their lives, they cannot see who Jesus is. But why does God allow this?

It is impossible to explain this fully. However, God showed his immense love for us when he sent his Son to die for sinful humanity. Jesus is the one true light, but people preferred to live in darkness, so Jesus embraced the darkness until the light overcame it with his ultimate sacrifice of love.

Reflections

- Look up John 1:3–5. If we follow him, Jesus will illuminate our paths so that we do not lose our way. How much do you allow his light to shine into your life?
- Blow out the candle and see the room grow darker again. Determine today never to allow the influence of Jesus' light to grow dim in your life.

Day 3

The gate and the good shepherd

Read John 10. In this passage, Jesus refers to himself as both the gate for the sheep and the good shepherd. With the first image he is revealing that he is the only way 'sheep' can find safety.

The second image, the shepherd, is packed full of clues to his character. Looking after sheep could be a dangerous business: the shepherd was responsible for each one and had to ward off any threats such as wolves, as well as working in all weather conditions.

Think about David from the Old Testament. As a young man, he was devoted to his sheep and protected them from lions and bears (see 1 Samuel 17). He knew how to use his weapons well and used them to kill Goliath. Being a shepherd was not for the faint-hearted!

Because a shepherd spends so much time with them, his sheep come to know his voice and trust him enough to follow wherever he takes them. Jesus is making a huge claim—that his disciples know him and hear his voice, and that he gives them eternal life.

Reflections

- Do an internet search on the phrase 'shepherds in biblical times'. Note particularly their standing in society and what they were expected to do. What further insights does this give you about Jesus?
- How well do you know Jesus' voice? What noisy distractions can you move out of the way in order to hear it better today?

Day 4

The resurrection and the life

Read John 11. Take some time to imagine what it would be like to be Martha or Mary. Jesus had been away when their brother Lazarus died, and they felt that if he had been there, he could have stopped Lazarus dying. And yet Jesus comes and comforts them, even crying himself. He indicates to Martha that her brother will rise again, which, understandably, she doesn't fully comprehend. Before he carries out his miracle, he responds to Martha's comment: 'I know he will rise again in the resurrection at the last day' by saying: 'I am the resurrection and the life. He who believes in me will live, even though he dies; and whoever lives and believes in me will never die' (vv. 24–25). What a powerful statement! He even asks her whether she believes it.

Jesus here is offering life for the body but also for the soul—this is future hope that can be guaranteed only by him who has ultimate authority. In a revelatory act, Jesus raises Lazarus from the dead, proving his power over all things. He again refers to the need for faith: 'Did I not tell you that if you believed, you would see the glory of God?' (v. 40).

Reflection

• Do an internet search for images of 'resurrection' and spend time contemplating one or two of the pictures you find.

Day 5

The way, the truth and the life—and the true vine

Read John 14—15. Jesus is talking to his disciples, not long before he is arrested. In John 14:6 Jesus says, 'I am the way, the truth and the life. No one comes to the Father except through me.' He is stating that he is the complete revelation of God to humanity, and through the way of suffering will bring life to all who believe.

The chapter goes on to link faith and obedience again, and then, at the start of chapter 15, Jesus says, 'I am the true vine, and my Father is the gardener' (15:1). This vivid pictorial language echoes the Old Testament idea of Israel being a vine/vineyard (see Psalm 80:8–16; Isaiah 5:1–7; Ezekiel 15:1–6; 19:10–14). Jesus was the true vine while Israel had fallen short. The gardener, the Father, cares for the vine, which shows the closeness of their relationship.

This love relationship is echoed in the love Jesus has for his disciples, and the command he gives them to remain in his love (John 15:4) and to love others.

Reflections

- If you are a gardener, think about why you prune. Even though it can seem painful, God's pruning in our lives is so that we can bear more fruit. (If you are not a gardener, do an internet search on 'pruning' to learn more about it.)
- There is such richness in the descriptions in these chapters. If you are artistic, try drawing a response. Alternatively, try writing a prayer or poem.

Saturday

Community activity

Jesus said he was the light of the world. He also taught that Christians are light, and we are encouraged to let our light shine before other people in order to draw them towards God (see Matthew 5:14–16—Paul also teaches something similar in Ephesians 5:8–10). Why not put together a presentation for the front of your church that focuses on this, including images and items that people can take away to remind them of the light, such as a small candle? Alternatively, you could spend time together brainstorming what you could do to let your light shine more brightly as a small group in your neighbourhood. Perhaps you could invite your neighbours for a barbecue during the summer, or offer to help with a DIY project?

Sunday

Reflective activity

Each aspect of Jesus' identity will begin to change us from the inside out as we open ourselves up to him more. Every one of the seven 'I am' statements therefore has a potential impact on our lives. Reflect on how much they have shaped who you are. Are there any that you would like to have more impact on you? Pray through your response today.

Review

We have seen how Jesus used his 'I am' sayings to reveal more about his divine nature to those around him. He often drew on imagery that would be familiar to them, but sometimes turned it on its head. Even though these sayings were some of the clearest claims he made about himself, most of the people who listened to him either didn't understand or chose to reject his meaning. We can still learn much about his nature and our standing as Christians through these sayings today. They show us how he wants us to depend on him and have faith in him, acting with absolute love and obedience.

Week 6
Meeting with Jesus

Overview

Anyone who truly meets with Jesus comes away changed. That's the same today as it was during the time he walked on earth. This week we are going to look at how, for some, a direct encounter means immediate change while, for others, it takes a journey of faith. We will look at both biblical and modern-day examples.

Day 1 (group session)

As John Drane says in *Introducing the New Testament* (Lion Hudson, 2010), in all four Gospels Jesus is presented as someone who was more interested in people than in ideas. He was impatient with the theological hair-splitting of religious experts and did not care to engage much in abstract debates, nor was he particularly interested in intellectual knowledge for its own sake. His whole life was focused on people and their needs.

The Gospels paint many vivid thumbnail sketches of Jesus at work among people—drinking with them, in casual conversations in fields and marketplaces—always with a view to bringing healing and renewal into their lives, as he pointed them to God and the kingdom. The fact that Jesus engaged in so many 'ordinary' things marked him out as different from other religious teachers.

Meeting Jesus makes a difference

Watch the video about a Jew who found Jesus. He explains how it was a process for him: www.foundations21.net/jesus

Now spend just a few minutes sharing your personal testimonies of how you came to meet Jesus for the first time. Was it a journey over a long period of time or a single event that drew you to him?

Meeting Jesus means meeting the truth

John's Gospel tells us how meeting with Jesus reveals certain truths to us. Chapter 4 contains many of these, including:

- Jesus is both human and divine (vv. 7–10)
- Jesus alone is able to give eternal life (vv. 11–14)

- Jesus gently wants to uncover all the secrets and lies of our lives, to replace them with his truth (vv. 15–19)
- Jesus knows the Father—and what it is truly to love and worship him—through the Holy Spirit (vv. 20–24)
- Jesus is the Messiah humanity has been waiting for (vv. 25–26)
- When we enter into the truth of this relationship, we are able to invite others to 'come and see' him for themselves (vv. 28–30)
- There are many people ready to hear the gospel—some may have been prepared for the good news by others before us (vv. 31–38)
- When others enter into the truth of a personal relationship with Jesus, that has to be unique to them (v. 42)

Group activities

- Look at the testimonies of what it means to people to be a Christian today: www.foundations21.net/jesus
- Discuss their stories. Can you relate to any of them?

Meeting Jesus means encountering his love

Jesus always reaches out in love, through his meeting of people's physical and spiritual needs, but also through his challenges. He wants us to know the Father and enjoy the new life we can have through his ultimate act of love.

Group activities

Get into twos and threes and answer the following questions:

- What do you love about Jesus at this moment?
- How have you seen the love of Jesus in your life?
- How has Jesus' love affected you, in the way you relate to others?

Reaching out to those deemed unlovely

Jesus sought out people whom other rabbis of his time would have tried to avoid (see Luke 19:10). How many examples of this can you remember in the Bible? Start by looking up the following:

- John 4:3–41 (foreigners)
- Matthew 4:23–25; 8:14; 9:35; 14:14; Mark 1:29–34; 3:1–5; 6:56; John 5:1–17 (the sick)
- Mark 5:21–43; Luke 7:11–17; 7:36–50; 10:38–42 (women)
- Matthew 4:23–25; 8:16; Mark 1:21–28; 6:13 (those who were demon-possessed)
- Mark 10:13–16 (children)
- Luke 7:36–39; Matthew 9:9–13 (sinners)

Questions for discussion

- Are there any people whom you try to avoid?
- To whom do you think Jesus is calling you to be an example of his love?

Day 2

Your own personal journey

Today, concentrate on thinking about how you met Jesus and on the main aspects of the character of Jesus that you have seen so far. In reality, Jesus Christ is so beautiful and magnificent that we can see him only, as Paul puts it, in a clouded mirror (1 Corinthians 13:12). When we are with Jesus forever we will see him face to face. Even so, there may have been special moments or seasons in your life when you have glimpsed a particular 'face of Jesus' more clearly. Focus on those today.

Reflections

- Write down your own journey of faith, adding in as few or as many moments as you remember that are part of your unfolding story with Jesus up to this point. For example, you may have met Jesus as 'friend' early on, whereas your meeting with 'the Jesus who heals' may have come much later. Be true to your 'face-to-face' meetings and relationship with Jesus at various points. The significance of this activity is that you can identify 'who Jesus was' at the different stages of your faith journey. He remains the same Jesus—the One who has loved, met and called you, but you may see 'who Jesus is' differently today from the way you did at the start.
- Watch the video about being on a faith journey, and make the prayer your own: www.foundations21.net/jesus

Day 3

A dramatic conversion

Read Acts 9:1–20. Paul met Jesus in a vision on the road to Damascus. He was travelling to seek permission to persecute the Christians, as he believed they were wrong in their claims. God arrested him dramatically, asked him why he was persecuting him and blinded him.

Here is how a humbled Paul may have described what happened next. Try to imagine the scene:

I was blind for three days afterwards. Then a disciple of Jesus called Ananias came and laid hands on my eyes and I was able to see again. He was brave, because I had come to Damascus to destroy the church and people like him. But out of his bravery and generosity to me, I felt, as I had never done before, the overwhelming love of God, and I knew that I had come home.

Reflections

- Can you remember a moment of elation when you understood what God had done for you?
- Think of something you can do to help someone on their 'Damascus Road' or their more gradual 'Emmaus Road' (see Luke 24:13–35)
- Read the Starfish Story (see www.foundations21.net/jesus). Respond in prayer.

Day 4

The woman at the well

Read John 4:1–42. This story reveals why Jesus was so captivating to those he met, and how he took the time to meet each one.

It was unusual enough that a religious teacher like Jesus should take a woman seriously, but this one was a Samaritan, a member of a group who were hated more than most by Jewish people.

She had also had a lot of experience with men, and possibly suffered much abuse, so could have been wary of him. Jesus knew he was speaking with a doubly disadvantaged person. So where did he begin? First, he revealed that he had a need: he was desperately thirsty. It was a need that she could meet, so he asked if she would share her water with him.

This placed him in a position of weakness, but by doing so he affirmed her value as a person. Right away she recognised something unusual was happening: this was to be a two-way conversation.

Jesus was a listener; not only that, he was prepared to follow her agenda. He did not focus on communicating a set of abstract ideas but on the questions the woman asked. Jesus always addressed people at their point of need. He was not primarily message-centred, but people-centred.

Reflection

- Do you tend to focus on getting the message across rather than listening to the person? What steps could you take to change that, and what have you learned from Jesus' approach?

Day 5

Meetings often resulted in miracles

As Jesus met people at their point of need, this sometimes resulted in miracles. He did not do these to impress the crowd, but because he was moved with compassion by the condition of those in need, or because they demonstrated extraordinary or unexpected faith.

'At no time did Jesus try to compete with the contemporary miracle-workers by using a magical formula or esoteric language to achieve his ends' (Michael Keene, *Lion Access Guides: Jesus*, Lion Hudson, 2002). Jesus' miracles were performed by the power of the Spirit.

Matthew's Gospel is full of examples of his healing miracles (see Matthew 8—9). Here is a list of some of the headings from those chapters (NIV): Jesus heals a man with leprosy, The faith of the centurion, Jesus heals many, Jesus restores two demon-possessed men, Jesus forgives and heals a paralysed man, The calling of Matthew, Jesus raises a dead girl and heals a sick woman, Jesus heals the blind and the mute.

Reflections

- Choose one or two examples of miracles to read and ponder.
- Watch the video about the blind man (see www.foundations21. net/jesus). Think how he must have felt, and how those around him must have felt too!
- Have you ever experienced a miracle or heard of one? Remind yourself what happened.
- What sort of impact do you think it would have on your community if something like this happened there today?

Saturday

Community activity

Few people outside the church are put off Christianity by the person and message of Jesus. In fact, many who express dissatisfaction with the church as an institution point to Jesus as someone to admire and respect. Do you think Jesus can speak to people through the image that is portrayed of him in culture outside the church?

Damaris has an online resource full of ideas on connecting Jesus' message with popular culture: see www.foundations21.net/jesus. Spend some time discussing them with people from your church to see if you can utilise any.

Sunday

Reflective activity

Jesus' power is just as alive now as it was in biblical times. He has supernatural powers far greater than we can imagine. How have you experienced the power of Jesus in your life, or seen other people influenced by him? What other powers do you believe are in the world today, and how can you know that Jesus' power is stronger than these?

Listen to the story of a woman meeting Jesus through intense suffering: www.foundations21.net/jesus

How do you respond to this?

Review

We have seen how Jesus' desire was—and still is—to meet people where they are. He often dealt with their physical needs and went on to minister to their spiritual ones. A dramatic meeting with Jesus may result in instant conversion, but sometimes people are on a journey towards him, and it takes time for them to recognise and accept him. Jesus' miracles, and indeed everything he did, were done in the power of the Spirit. That same Spirit is with us today, and he has called us to be his witnesses to those around us. Are you helping to point the way to Jesus simply through the way that you live your everyday life?

Week 7
Following Jesus

Overview

This week we are going to focus on what it means to follow Jesus. We will look at the first disciples and at what Jesus called them to be and do. This should also have an impact on our lives today, as we have been commissioned to continue with the same mission they had. How do we live day to day in the light of this?

Day 1 (group session)

Watch the video in which believers describe how they feel about Jesus: www.foundations21.net/jesus. (We watched a small section of this in Week 1.) Now spend some time describing what being a disciple of Jesus means for each of you today.

The first disciples were with him all the time, listening and learning. We, as his disciples, can do the same. We can choose to trust him and follow his lead in our lives. Becoming a follower of Jesus Christ means increasingly taking on certain responsibilities. One is to be watching for signs of God at work around us. Another is to be open to accepting the truth that part of God's work is to reveal himself to others through us.

Group activity

In threes or fours, take it in turns to try the following: you're at a party. An intense person comes up to you and asks, 'Who are you?' They don't just want to know your name. They want to know how you see yourself. What do you say? What are the top five things you would use to define your identity? Here are some suggestions, but feel free to use your own:

- Job, work or employment
- Hobbies and leisure pursuits
- Education and skills
- Racial group and ethnicity
- Political affiliations
- Religion and faith
- Group memberships or associations
- Personality type

After you have all completed this, think about the following questions individually:

- How long would it be before you revealed that you are a Christian? What words would you use to tell them about your commitment to being a disciple of Jesus Christ?
- What would you be thinking inside, as you tell this other person who you are?
- Now compose a written prayer in response to hearing God ask you: 'Who do you say YOU are?' Share them among your smaller groups.

Why are we called disciples?

It is interesting to note that the New Testament refers to followers of Jesus as 'believers' 26 times, 'Christians' only three times, but 'disciples' over 260 times. So what does the word 'disciple' mean? It comes from the Greek *mathetes*, which means 'learner' or 'pupil', and its verb form, *manthano*, means 'to learn'. Discipleship is about learning and also passing on that knowledge to others.

Whole-life discipleship

The phrase 'whole-life discipleship' refers to the fact that we choose to bring every area of our lives under the leadership of Christ: there are no spiritual/secular divides, no private areas in which we do not want to allow his good news to make a difference. As we can see from the Gospels, if we are going to be members of the kingdom of God, we have to acknowledge that the king of that kingdom is interested in every area of our lives.

Revealing himself through people

Here are stories from some of the Old Testament prophets, which show ways in which God chose to reveal himself through his people. Some are strange and others comforting:

- Isaiah 38:1–8
- Jeremiah 13:1–11
- Ezekiel 24:15–18
- Daniel 6:13–24
- Hosea 3:1–3

Group activities

- Write down a brief story of how you've seen God at work in someone else. Make sure that this is a story from outside the direct life of the church. It may be from work, a social group or an everyday occurrence in your neighbourhood.
- Write a second short story about an event that showed God at work in your life.
- How do you feel about having the responsibility of being someone who is called to live out God's Word?

Day 2

Taking the family likeness

Read Romans 8:15–28 and Ephesians 1:5. Once we've made the decision to follow Christ, we are adopted into his family and become co-heirs. In Roman law, an adult who wanted an heir and someone to carry on the family name adopted a male as his son.

The imagery of sonship used in the New Testament refers to all believers in Jesus—both men and women. Spend a few minutes thinking about the extraordinary idea that we are joint heirs with Christ of all that God has to give.

If your parents hurt or abused you in any way, thank God that he loves you in a way no earthly parent ever could. If you have been blessed with parents who love you and have won your respect, thank God and ask him to show you how to express your appreciation to them.

Being in a family or other grouping requires discipline—Jesus' disciples and the early Christians discovered this! Being family also means accepting each other even when we fail.

Reflections

- How well do you feel you are fitting into God's family and appreciating its values?
- At Jesus' baptism, God the Father said that Jesus is his Son in whom he is well pleased. Imagine you can hear his voice saying to you: 'You are my son/daughter.' How does that make you feel? How does it change the way you think about yourself?

Day 3

Calling his disciples

Go to Google Maps, put in your postcode, then click on 'satellite' to see where you are. Now zoom out, until you are on the map of the whole world. Jesus called his disciples from a little village beside the Sea of Galilee. Do a search for this. Then God made them fishers of people—following Jesus placed them on a much larger map.

Read Matthew 4:18–22. Several of Jesus' twelve disciples said 'yes' to following him almost on the spur of the moment. No doubt they had seen or heard something of Jesus, but it is still amazing that they left their nets—and everything else they had known—immediately when he said, 'Follow me.' Only as time went on did they realise how much they were committed to a whole new way of life.

It is in the later chapters of the Gospels that we find them grasping the full significance of Jesus as Lord and Master, typified in Thomas's words after the resurrection: 'My Lord and my God' (John 20:28). The same is true of many of today's disciples.

Reflections

- When do you think the disciples fully accepted the cost of discipleship?
- Have you had to make any sacrifices because of following Jesus? Do you think you have fully counted the cost of discipleship?
- Did you know that 'Lord' is used about 50 times in Matthew's Gospel? There's an old saying: 'If Jesus isn't Lord of all, he's not Lord at all.'

Day 4

What Jesus expects of his followers

Being a disciple of Jesus means obeying him wholeheartedly, and living a life of sacrifice as he did. It can be costly, but read the following suggestion:

I think once you understand that his authority is not that of a tyrant or a despot but of a lover who wants the very best for his people then you very very gladly surrender to it and revel in it.
MICHAEL GREEN, IN VIDEO ON WWW.FOUNDATIONS21.NET

Here are some of Jesus' commands to his followers:

- Believe I am who I claim to be (John 3:16; 5:24; 6:29; 11:25–26; 12:46)
- Have faith (Mark 4:39–40; 10:51–52; 11:22–24; Luke 8:48)
- Love and obey God (Matthew 7:21; 22:37–40)
- Love and obey me (John 8:31–32; 14:15; Matthew 16:24–26)
- Love one another (John 13:34; 15:12, 17; Matthew 22:39)
- Forgive one another (Matthew 18:21–2; Mark 11:25; Luke 6:37)
- Draw close to me (Matthew 11:28–30; John 7:37–38; 14:21)

Note how many of these are based on love and on preferring others to ourselves—which Jesus modelled himself.

Reflections

- What principles have you built your life on?
- Reflect again on Jesus' commands. How do your principles relate to what he said and did? (Look up Luke 22:24–27.)
- Is there anything that you have heard God telling you to do recently, but have not followed through on?

Day 5

Continuing the mission

Listen to the song by Graham Kendrick, 'In you we live', and reflect on the words that are printed on the site: www.foundations21.net/jesus

Read Matthew 28:18–20. This is known as 'the great commission'. Before Jesus ascended into heaven, he made it clear to his followers that he was passing them the baton of telling the world his message. That is still true today, as God calls all Christians to follow him and build his eternal kingdom by reaching out to others with his love so that they have the chance to respond to him for themselves.

Maybe God is asking you to talk to a non-Christian friend about Christ, or perhaps he wants you to take his message to the young people of your community, or it could be that God is sending you out on an overseas mission. Whatever the situation, sometimes we have to go outside our comfort zones in order for other people to know that Jesus is Lord.

Reflections

- Watch the video 'Holistic gospel' (see www.foundations21.net/jesus) and reflect on how you feel about it. Do you agree with what is being said? If so, think about how that should affect your life.
- Who are the people around the world who are waiting to hear about Jesus Christ?
- And who are the people near you who are waiting to hear about Jesus?
- Where do you think God is sending you with his message of good news today?

Saturday

Community activity

Discuss together how your church shows other people in the community that you are followers of Jesus. Remember he went to people where they were, and met both their physical and their spiritual needs. Is your church involved, for example, in any inter-church initiatives such as food banks, shelters for the homeless or prison ministry? Brainstorm ways in which your church could help those in the surrounding area. For example, if you have nursing homes near the church and people who are able to visit on a regular basis, consider setting up a befriending scheme.

Sunday

Reflective activity

How have you shown that you are a follower of Jesus this week? Reflect back on:

- What you have said to Jesus
- What Jesus has said to you
- How you have trusted him
- How you have obeyed him
- What you have said about Jesus
- What you have done in Jesus' name
- In whom you have seen Jesus
- When you have asked 'What would Jesus do?' (WWJD?) to help you respond to a situation appropriately

If you wish, create a WWJD reminder. You could make a poster or set the motto as your screen saver.

Review

We have seen that becoming a follower of Christ is both a privilege and a costly decision. The good news is that we become heirs of all that God has for his children—but we need to learn to open ourselves up to his rule and reign in every area of our lives. And his church is the means by which God spreads his message, so we also have a responsibility to share the wonderful new life we've found in him with others, otherwise they may not get another chance to hear and respond. What a sobering thought. Let's live our lives as dedicated disciples of Christ.

Bibliography

T.D. Alexander, Brian S. Rosner, (editors), *New Dictionary of Theology*, The Essential IVP Reference Collection, (Intervarsity Press, 2000)

John Drane, *Introducing the New Testament* (Lion Hudson, 2010)

John Eddison, *Newness of Life* (BRF, 1999)

Dick France, *Mark*, The People's Bible Commentary, (BRF, 1998)

Rob Frost, *Jesus in the Third Millennium* (BRF, 2000)

Joel B. Green, et al. (editors), *The Dictionary of Jesus and the Gospels*, The Essential IVP Reference Collection (Intervarsity Press, 1992)

Michael Keene, *Lion Access Guides: Jesus* (Lion Hudson, 2002)

John Proctor, *Matthew*, The People's Bible Commentary (BRF, 2001)

Lenad Ryke, et al. (editors), *The Dictionary of Biblical Imagery*, The Essential IVP Reference Collection (Intervarsity Press, 1998)

Linda Smith, William Raeper, *Luke: A Gospel for Today* (Lion Children's Books, 1989)

Tom Wright, *Following Jesus* (SPCK, 1994)

Tom Wright, *The Original Jesus* (Lion Books, 1997)

www.allaboutjesuschrist.org/gospel-of-luke.htm

www.jesuscentral.com/ji/jesus-parables-teachings/jesus-commands.php

www.lifehouse.org/tracts/jmwhythesonofgodbecamethesonofman.htm

http://preachersfiles.com/i-am-the-bread-of-life/

http://mb-soft.com/believe/text/christol.htm

About Foundations21

Foundations21 **www.foundations21.net** is BRF's free online resource for Christian life-long learning and discipleship, and has provided much of the material for this book. It's a unique resource for people to use alongside the Bible to enable them to move forward in their discipleship of Jesus Christ.

It provides:

- 12 themes to explore
- 3500 pages of content
- over 6 hours of video
- links to over 7500 other websites
- reflection exercises
- daily devotional material

and much, much, more!

If you go online at www.foundations21.net, you will be able to use more material in your chosen learning style. To find out which your learning style is, do the quiz on the homepage.